The Guide to Navigating YOUR PM Career

Janice Y. Rodgers, PMP
&
Brenda K. Williams, PMP

ISBN:150058276X
ISBN-13:9781500582760

DEDICATION

This book is dedicated to all the PMs and aspiring PMs we have had the pleasure to work alongside. We hope the best for you in your career transitions!

Best of Luck to you all!

Janice & Brenda

Table of Contents

Introduction

Another year has come and gone...did you accomplish all that you planned? As Your PM Assistant (YPMA), we want to share with you thoughts, questions, and ideas that will help you reflect on your accomplishments and focus on where you're headed. As the old saying goes ... how do you know where you're headed unless you know where you've been (or something like that ☺)? Our goal is to help you with an "YPMA" - Your Project Management Assessment career development plan. This process will help you get and stay on the right track to PM (**P**roject **M**anager - **P**rogram **M**anager - **P**ortfolio **M**anager) career success. As we go forward, the letters PM will be used interchangeably.

As you go through this book, you will see sections that with a marker that states "Take Notes". This is your opportunity to STOP READING, REFLECT, and DOCUMENT your situation as part of Your PM Assessment. It's important to take the time to reflect as you progress through this assessment, so you can return to your notes and reassess your progress. Remember, this is all about YOU!

YPMA - Development Plan & Career Considerations

Your PM Assistant is here for you as your personal coach. As with all coaching, the end result is about moving you to a better place and training you to improve yourself through clear instruction and progressive improvements. As a part of this coaching, this book will begin with the basics of every improvement plan. Understand how you want to meet your goal by asking the key questions ...What, When, Where, Who, Why and How. These key questions are then structured into the Top 25 notable lessons for PM progression to further help you assess your career. Now let's get started!

Why Project Management?

1. Why did you become a PM? Why do you want to become a PM? Are you committed to excellence in the craft of Project Management?

Project Management is a field that requires tenacity, discipline and advanced training. There are many who call themselves project managers but don't have the foundation to execute a plan to success. There are also those who execute project plans on a consistent basis with success and do not have the title of a PM or have any certification designations. So, think about why you want to be a project manager and then consider if you have the skills, ability and commitment.

Reasons to become a PM:

(PM = Project / Program / Portfolio Manager)

- To earn more money

- To experience more challenging assignments

- To use your organizational skills

- To enhance your leadership skills

- To reinforce your planning skills

- To strengthen your facilitation skills

- To elevate your negotiation skills

- To advance your career

- To diversify your skillset

What is your reason for becoming a Project / Program / Portfolio Manager?

I am amazed that many of my fellow co-workers who are in the PM Field did not start with the goal of one day becoming a PM. It is something that has evolved for most. Let's take Ms. B for example. As a junior in college she took her first class in the introduction to computers. She fell in love with computers and all she could think of was one day becoming a software engineer. Ms. B loved the fact that each day of work would be different. She could solve complex algorithms and problems day after day and get paid for it. The key for her was that she liked to analyze things and solve problems. As she went through the ranks from Software Developer, to Senior Software Developer, to Team Leader she got further from the things she loved - analyzing and solving technical challenges. Her journey from Team Leader to Functional Manager to Project Manager was a very gratifying journey. As a Project Manager, she is now back to analyzing and solving problems but of a different nature. Everyone has their own path..choose yours!

2. Where are you on the PM Career Path?

Depending on the industry, the PM progression may look something like what is shown below.

Project Coordinator	→	Asst. Project Manager	= Entry Level
Project Manager	→	Sr. Project Manager	= Professional Level
Program Manager	→	Sr. Program Manager	= Management Level
Portfolio Manager	→	Sr. Portfolio Manager	= Executive Level

The previous progression is a sample depiction of a PM's progression in an IT organization. Depending on the industry and department, the titles may also be slightly different. However, the levels should be similar.

The education requirements may also be different depending on which transition you are making. Not all companies require a degree/certification. So if you have been with an organization for a number of years, they are more likely to allow a lateral move with a proven track record (without the degree requirements). If you have met the organization requirements, you may be able to post for the position. When entering a new organization on the other hand, the minimum requirements are typical of what is required.

Project Coordinators and Assistant Project Managers are typically resources who are assisting the project manager to complete tasks as assigned. They are responsible to compile project status reports, coordinate project schedules (familiarity with MS project is desired), arrange project meetings, and identify and resolve simple technical problems. They also identify and analyze system requirements and define project scope, requirements, and deliverables for projects that are simple to moderate in complexity. Additionally, they will coordinate project activities and ensure all project phases are documented appropriately. An example of this would be the follow-up and documentation of status reports and milestone achievements. This level typically requires an associate's degree and 2-4 years of experience in the field or in a related area. They should also be familiar with standard concepts, practices, and procedures within a particular field/industry. They should rely on experience and judgment to plan and accomplish goals. They should perform a variety of tasks with a degree of creativity - latitude is required. They typically report to a supervisor or manager.

Project Manager and Senior Project Managers are typically responsible for managing projects from initiation to go-live/deployment. During the implementation, they are responsible for confirming that the requirements (approved scope) are documented, tested, and that all milestones are met with the scheduled timeframe. They will also work to ensure that customers are trained. This position usually requires a bachelor's or master's degree (or equivalent work experience) and anywhere from 5-10 years of experience in the field or in a related area.

Certification is desirable at this level and the PM is more likely to be responsible for multiple complex projects concurrently.

Program Manager and Senior Program Managers

typically have the overall responsibility and accountability for managing projects and programs across business and technical areas with a variation of risk, complexity and duration. The primary goal of this position is to efficiently manage the time, cost, scope (aka: triple constraints) quality and integration for multiple projects and/or programs across the organization. The Program Manager relies on the experience they have obtained to this point in their careers to communicate technical issues to a variety of stakeholders including project team members and management. This PM is responsible for stakeholder engagement, strategic initiatives, leadership and more complex communications.

While they are responsible for more complexities, they are also leading Project Managers and possibly other Program Managers. Depending on the organization, they can be responsible for Project portfolio risk analysis, assessment, planning and will interface with internal and external stakeholders. They must have managed large scale projects, shown expertise in a documented project management methodology (from initiation through closure), and be able to delegate budgetary responsibility, and scope authority.

This position would require a bachelor's or master's degree (or equivalent work experience) and typically 10+ years of experience in the field or in a related area. Most times requiring PMP® certification. This level is more likely to be responsible for multiple more complex projects concurrently.

Portfolio Manager and Senior Portfolio Managers are typically leaders who are responsible for setting strategic direction for the department including planning and implementation of new technology solutions, as well as setting company policy and procedures for the organization. This level will evaluate, define and play a key role in prioritizing user needs as well as establishing project objective and accountabilities. This could include new software application development, purchase of software packages and maintenance of existing systems, management of systems administration and help desk efforts, including system security and service level agreements (SLA) related to each. The portfolio plans are on a high level for the deployment of new technology solutions, consideration of company's budget guidelines and impact on users and long term goals of the organization. They have total responsibility for the staff which includes the day-to-day management oversight and training where needed; including contractors or outsourced/managed services.

This position would require a bachelor's or master's degree (or equivalent work experience) and typically 12+ years of experience in the field or in a related area with advanced education and or advanced certification. This level is more likely to report to the CIO, with regular communications with senior management.

Bottom line, each of these levels will need to have many of the same skills but require those skills being refined and perfected as you move up the ladder in your career path. The area's most notable are: leadership skills, experience in design, development, and maintenance of enterprise level data systems, implementation of systems, understanding the project life cycle, project management experience, excellent written and oral communication skills, excellent time management and organizational skills, and the ability to adapt to a fast paced, constantly changing environment. One of the things sure to note is industry experience: government, manufacturing, insurance, financial, construction, engineering, defense, non-for-profit, evangelical, etc.

No matter where you are on the PM career path, the next level up will surely provide you with more of a challenge. That additional challenge can include more communications, more accountability, more responsibility and more leadership responsibilities on the horizon.

What level are you on today? Is your current role challenging? If not, are you ready to move to the next level? What do you need to do to get there? When do you plan to do it?

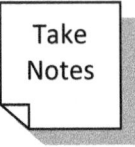

When Is It Time for a Change?

3. <u>As you progress in your PM career, will your growth help you achieve success on your projects? If not now, when?</u>

Your success is unfortunately not guaranteed because you are promoted from one level to the next. You would hope that you have the skills and ability to do well in the next level, but it is not a given. Consequently, it is up to you to enhance your skills and abilities to ensure that your competencies are elevated.

It is important to know that in a Project Management career 80 – 90% of the job is communication; requiring you to get better and better at written and oral communication. Communication is about the sending and receiving of information; including the ability to disseminate the information to the most appropriate people at the appropriate time. These enhanced communications can be elevated by formal education, Toastmasters®, holding leadership positions within associations and organizations and more. It is up to you to get what you need to be the best you can become.

Formal education can come in the form of post-secondary education, targeted courses, online courses, internal company education, webinars, seminars, conferences and more.

Volunteering at local organizations (church, not-for-profit, associations, etcetera.) can also help your communication skills; while you also give back to the community.

You are responsible to assess your needs and target the avenue that bests provides you with the path to enhance your skills. The question is when are you going to do it?

What areas (skills, abilities, knowledge) do you need to grow in?

When (realistically of course) do you expect for this activity to happen?

4. Are you CPAM® → PMP® → PgMP® Certified? Do you have other certifications? When will be a good time to go to the next level?

If you are not familiar with these certifications please go to www.PMI.org for additional information.

Once you have mastered your current level, it is a good time to think of the educational direction you want to go and how to get there. If advanced education is the key, formal education through post-secondary level institutions or advanced certification in Project Management can help.

If you are looking to change jobs, your current employer may/may not require certification. Review the requirements that are provided for your organization's internal posting process.

If you are going to another company, additional certifications can help give you an edge over your competition. Take a look at some of the jobs that are posted online to get an idea of what education requirements are required (as a minimum) for you to apply at other organizations.

Certification is a gauge of competency for the PM field. Having your certification means that you have knowledge and training on a particular level. Various project management certifications (CPAM®/ PMP®/ PgMP®) can be obtained through the Project Management Institute or post-secondary institutions. Please go to www.pmi.org or search the internet for local colleges and/or organizations that offer this type of training for more information.

What are your educational goals…that will help you attain the next level in your career progression?

Who Are Your Supporters?

5.   <u>Do you have a role model or mentor?   What is</u>

<u>important to you in a career role model? Is the job they</u>

<u>have one you want?   Are they in the PM field or on</u>

<u>another career track?</u>

The first part of this question is the most important. If you don't currently have a mentor or coach helping to navigate your career, the probability of you being successful will be limited. It is always important to open your mind to new ideas and keep conversations about your career open and continuous.

Having the confidence of a mentor allows you to ask questions, get guidance, and expand your knowledge of various options. If your mentor has a successful career in your specific profession, even better. That person can give you an understanding of their experiences and can help you in the process to navigate through the sometimes complicated career path options. Of course, you don't have to have a mentor to be successful…but it surely won't hurt! ☺

6. <u>What person in the field of Project Management would you most want to emulate? Are they within your current organization? What is the possibility of them being your coach or mentor?</u>

Take
Notes

This is always a great topic. Who do you want to model your career after? Who do you feel respect for and who most closely aligns to your integrity and morals? Who would you select to show you the way?

Okay, even though these are some heady questions, they don't have to be. Think about them, identify someone in your organization or outside that has risen to a level that you deem successful and ask them to lunch or for a quick 30 minute meeting. You will be surprised how many people will accept your request and are genuinely honored and willing to help.

Remember, you are looking for someone that will be there for you and can make a commitment of at least a quarterly meeting to understand your goals and provide guidance on your path to achieve them. If you do find your "perfect" mentor and they say no, don't be discouraged and don't take it personal. For whatever reason, that person wasn't the "right" fit for you. My personal feeling is that if it is meant to be it will happen.

You need someone that will commit and truly try to understand where you are going and help you get there. There are many mentors that are just waiting to be asked. Find the one that's right for you!

What Competencies Matter?

7. <u>What competencies (attitudes, abilities, skills, knowledge) are important in your current position? What competencies would you like to add/improve upon?</u>

Take Notes

Competencies are those behaviors that PMs possess that are considered essential to become successful in this field. We will review some, but not all competencies that could be considered. Review the postings at your organization to determine what competencies are most important for you now. We will review a short list that is in alphabetical order so that there is no assumption as to one being more or less important than another.

28

These competencies can be used to evaluate current PM's on an annual basis, for screening perspective candidates or providing a benchmark for expected behaviors.

Communication is the exchange of information in all directions using various media for delivery. Successful PMs communicate in a clear and concise manner both written and verbally. They are good listeners, and are able to progressively elaborate on a variety of topics both technically and operationally.

Customer Focus involves the successful PM managing the interactions between the customer and/or end user and all the stakeholders on the team. The customer can be in-house or external to the organization. In either case it is important to maintain consistent customer satisfaction.

Decision Making involves the judgment of the successful PM to determine the optimal choice among a variety of alternatives for a complex situation. The focus is to have the right decision made at the right time. The most important aspect is to delegate and escalate effectively and to ensure the successful implementation by following up in a timely manner.

Leadership is the motivation and inspiration of others. Successful PMs provide direction to their project team(s), have a positive attitude, work well under pressure, and are responsible/accountable for the results of their respective project team.

Negotiation involves the PM working with team members in adverse situations to ensure the outcome is a WIN-WIN solution. Successful PMs need to be objective and follow-up to ensure that the people issues are resolved in a positive manner so that the team remains harmonious.

Problem Solving involves the identification (what), triage (options to resolve) and correction or resolution (implementation) of complex problems. They can come in a variety of flavors. To name a few, they can be technical, managerial, resource, process, workflow and/or operational. Successful PMs have a documented approach that will identify the root cause in their problem solving process and provide timely feedback and resolutions.

Project Planning is a major role for the successful PM. Much of their time is dedicated to developing project plans, maintaining project plans and ensuring that the integration of tasks is complete. This will necessitate being familiar with a variety of tools that are used in the planning and reporting process. This information is translated in a number of ways that provides information to all stakeholders and in a variety of formats (i.e. status reports, presentations, process flows, etc.).

Team Management & Development involves the PMs formation and assimilation of the team towards a common goal. Successful PMs will ensure that all team members are identified and are provided the opportunity to be trained to the extent that they are capable of handling the tasks at hand. They will also work to keep the team encouraged and motivated so that the team performs at an optimal level. They will, many times, use team activities to ensure the assimilation and camaraderie happens for optimal performance.

Risk Management involves the successful PM working with the team to identify, analyze and document potential risks including steps for mitigation where necessary. Risk Management requires that contingencies and reserves are allocated as needed.

8. <u>What are your strengths as a PM?</u>

There are many tools and techniques to find out your strengths. These tools focus on finding out your strengths and can be used individually or in a team setting to understand the strengths of others. Search the web to find one that suits your needs.

List 5 attributes/characteristics you think are your strengths and another 5 that others would consider your strengths.

Take
Notes

What can you do to make your career more successful?

A wise woman once said to me…"You keep doing what you're doing, you'll keep getting what you're getting". Of course she was paraphrasing for Mr. Albert Einstein who said it another way where he defined insanity. He said, "Insanity: doing the same thing over and over again and expecting different results." Basically, this means you have to look at your career and learn how to improve yourself as well as your career progression by opening up yourself to new opportunities. New opportunities exist like, advanced training, leadership opportunities, a possible lateral move to learn different skills, building your network, taking on additional responsibilities, as well as joining professional associations. All of these improvements can make you more successful and force you to step out of your comfort zone and do something that really makes a difference to your career. Come on, what are you planning to do to really shake up your career and move it to the next level?

List ways that you can make your career more successful:

Take
Notes

9. What do you expect your career path to look like? Are you on track?

Do you want to be in management, a C-level executive, an entrepreneur, a program manager? What do you want your end game to look like? Where do you see yourself in 10, or 15 or even 20 years in your career? Once you have that vision of where you are headed, how do you need to navigate through your career to get there? One of the key things to think about is if you are on the right track. Are you on the right track for your dream job? Are you on the right track for your position? What is it that you want? You have to define this for yourself and then you can help shape your career into your dreams. Remember, no two people are alike...so in that vein, no two careers are alike. You have to find your way by looking at what works for you and your family. The only way to do this is to make sure you know where you want to go and you have a plan to get there. Earlier in this book, we showed you some typical career paths. Was there anything that resonated with you? Do you have a career path in your current company? If so, take some time to do the next exercise which focuses on looking at the career options in your organization and think through the types of roles and experience you need to take yourself to the next level. Whatever that level might be. Be sure to ask your coach/mentor for input in setting your goals.

Chart out the PM progression within your current organization and do an assessment to determine if you are on track. Are you on track? What's your next job? Do you currently have the skills to be competitive at your next position? If not, how will you

go about finding the skills and experiences you need?

When will you do this? Now's a good time!

Take
Notes

How Do I Advance My Career?

10. <u>Are there opportunities to advance in your current organization? If not, are you ready to pursue changes outside of your current organization?</u>

Change is a difficult thing. Sometimes when you're faced with the possibility of change you tend to procrastinate (even on a subconscious level). Take for instance thinking through moving to a new organization or even a new job. Does the thought of it scare you – deep down? Do you think about the fact you won't know anyone, you won't understand their processes, you won't understand their organization? These are common fears but you have to fight through them to take action on seriously considering opportunities to advance (inside and outside your current organization). Do this for me today. Look at the job opportunities in your organization. Look at the job opportunities outside your organization. Access your network on LinkedIn®, Twitter, Facebook, and all the other various professional and personal networking tools.

Look at the postings in your organization and search the internet for your next position. What did you find of interest? Is it worth looking at next steps?

Take Notes

<u>Do you need educational assistance to help you attain your aspirations? Certification, Degree, etc.</u>

Take
Notes

Obtaining more education in your chosen field will always be beneficial. It may not mean that you will get an immediate raise or promotion, but will set the stage for you to attain a higher level in the future. This is where your preparation meets opportunity to move you in a favorable direction.

You might think…I'm too old to go back to school. I would say unequivocally not true. You might say, I don't have time to go back to school, although this might be true, sometimes you have to make time for things that will benefit you and your family in the long run.   I know what you're thinking, education is expensive. Again, this is very true. However, there are options in education funding. You can check with your employer for employer funded options, you can check with the school you're interested in for options on financing, grant opportunities, or even scholarships. Even if you have to take one class at a time, getting your education and improving your skills is instrumental in staying relevant in this very competitive job market.

What is the next level you will need to attain in your career path? Do you need education to attain this next level? If so, what education do you need? What are some ideas on how to fund this education?

11. <u>How can you pursue additional tasks / more responsibilities that will provide more opportunities to advance?</u>

Take
Notes

There are times when your current position will not give you the exposure you need to attain your next position. So sometimes, you will have to look outside of your current situation to find other opportunities to keep you challenged. Let's talk about a few:

- Volunteer activities can help you hone and perfect your leadership skills. In the process, you will have the satisfaction of giving back to your community or specific cause and also have the opportunity to expand your network.

- Special Assignments can also give you exposure to other activities and individuals that you would not have otherwise met on your day-to-day path. Depending on the assignment, it can also help get you out of your comfort zone. You can ask your supervisor about opportunities that might exist within your organization. You will be surprised at the many ways that exist to expand your opportunities to advance that you might not have realized.

- Toastmasters® can help you with presentation skills, camaraderie, and provide a networking opportunity. This is a great organization that will do many things to help your confidence as well as expand your network.

- Associations like PMI® (Project Management Institute) will provide an opportunity for meeting others who share your same interests. They also have monthly meetings on topics of interest and other fun activities (cruises, conferences, meetings) that will be instrumental in helping you attain your career goals.

- Social networks like LinkedIn® provide a forum to stay connected to other professionals; use message boards to gain insight on special topics and they allow you to share your technical expertise.

Write down some ideas based on the above examples or come up with a few of your own that you think will give you an edge and open you up to new

opportunities and experiences.

Take
Notes

12. How can your mentor, coach, colleagues help you to attain the skills that you need?

Everybody needs someone they can talk to and confide in every so often, especially on sensitive topics that may be a new experience. Think about what your needs are as you do this assessment and come up with ways your mentor, coach or a colleague can help. A good way to do this outside of your brainstorming is to have your supervisor, colleagues, subordinates, etc. complete a 360 assessment on you. If you ever want some unbiased feedback, this is a great way to get the truth and get some great feedback on how people see you and understand where you might need some additional skills. Often we perceive ourselves as one way, and often others see us a completely different way. Take some time to find out where your skills might need sharpening or where your strengths might need further refinement.

What help do you need?

Take
Notes

13. How can you use social media to advance your career?

As a job seeker, what a marvelous tool we have to find a job these days. Social media can put you in contact with people that just 5 years ago you might not have a chance of knowing or keeping up with. Since my introduction to LinkedIn®, I have been reunited to coworkers that I knew over 20 years ago. We lost track after I or they moved away. That is no longer an issue when you have your network on LinkedIn®. The network goes with you wherever you go.

As an employer, social media is used to find a wide range of candidates with a variety of backgrounds. It has not totally taken the place of a resume but definitely provides an enormous amount of supplemental information. Members can endorse one another which give companies an opportunity to search for the specific skills and competencies they are looking for.

LinkedIn® also has a job board that provides you with a snapshot of positions based on your search criteria for opportunities in many places.

Join LinkedIn® today. If you are already a member enhance your profile for the ultimate benefit. What other social media can you use to help advance your career?

Take
Notes

14. <u>How can you use various tools available to help</u>

<u>you advance in your field?</u> <u>Books, webinars, e-</u>

<u>learning, brown bag/lunch & learns, association</u>

<u>presentations, user groups, networking</u>

Here are some thoughts on the many tools that you should be taking advantage of on a daily, weekly, or at least monthly basis:

- Books are always good food for thought. They can help in your advancement in many ways but two come to mind immediately. One way, you can acquire unprecedented amounts of knowledge by reading them. And two, you can pay it forward to your colleagues by writing one!

- Webinars come across my inbox on a daily basis that are beneficial in providing knowledge on competencies that you can use to advance your career. The good thing about webinars is that if you are not available for the live broadcast, many times you will still find them recorded and on the initiators website for you to view at your convenience.

- E-learning is a powerful tool that you can use at your convenience. My organization provides free classes that range from leadership, certification, to a wide variety of self- help organization specific topics. If you have the availability within your organization, there are usually a variety of options regarding project management. Not only do you have interim topics that can help in your job, there are also formal certifications you can obtain.

- Brown bag lunch and learns are convenient learning sessions that you can participate in while you eat your lunch. You have to eat, why not learn while you are doing it! ☺

- Association presentations typically provide a subject matter expertise on a variety of topics of interest. Check with your local associations (ex.www.pmi.org) to find topics that are of interest to you. You can also do an Internet search on local associations. If you don't find any, maybe it's time for you to put a presentation together and share it with others in your PM community. No matter what level you are, there is information you have learned that would be helpful to share with others.

- User groups are formed to assist like-minded individuals with a certain topic. There are many user groups for project management that can help you increase your skills within the field. Join one or even two!

- Networking is not only fun, it is essential. They say the worst time to look for a job is when you don't have one. Building a network will give you immediate access to hundreds if not thousands of individuals that can help you with a job search, information search and stay connected. On my LinkedIn® network new information is being shared every day that helps me stay tuned to the topics of interest within project management. So if you don't have a network, start today to build one.

15. Review the various tools and decide on at least three to help you advance in your career. What are they? Why did you pick those?

Food for Thought:

16. The life of a PM is built around their project plan. Create your own career plan to include action items for your career success.

17. Once you create your plan, update it as new information is available. You know the PM term – progressive elaboration (get the outline down and then fill in the details). At least review it on a quarterly or yearly basis and refine it as appropriate.

18. Align your personal goals with your annual review at work. While achieving the organizational goals make sure you include goals of personal satisfaction. Continuing education benefits your organization as well as yourself.

19. Share your expertise outside of work. Volunteer with user groups and/or associations. If you have challenges with public speaking or want to be more confident, join your local Toastmasters.

20. Communication is 85-90% of the PM's job. Always look for ways to enhance your communication skills. Public speaking, writing, negotiation and networking. If you are an introvert, look for activities that will draw you out.

21. Do a risk assessment on your career plan. No doubt you will find challenges along the way. The best way to ensure a successful career plan is to consider what can go wrong and decide on alternative paths you can take when necessary.

22. Keep a close connection to your fan club. They are your support group and want you to do well - your PM mentor, your PM coach, your PM champion. They will help you stay the course.

23. Don't become an extended visitor in your present position. When you stop being challenged or you are not happy in your current position, be accountable to yourself to make a true self-assessment and make a change when the time is right.

24. Last but not least....Give thanks to those who have helped you along the way. You never know when they won't be there for you to share. So share today and make a difference!

EXTRA TIP:

25. After all is said and done. Figure out how to pay it forward. You did not get to where you are by your lonesome. Someone somewhere saw the spark in your eye and helped you along the way. Do the same for another PM who is making their way!

Other Books by Rodgers & Williams

Project Management Made Easy

"A Week-in-the-Life", Understanding the role of a project manager!

Have you ever wanted to pick up a project management book that you could quickly understand? One that contains relevant business terminology and that actually takes you through a "week in the life" of a project manager? Then look no further!

Houston, Texas – 2013 - *A Week-in-the-Life, Understanding the role of a project manager* provides a quick and easy reference for all project managers. Want to start a project, but not sure if you have all the key areas covered? Look no more! This book is for you. Want to find some quick templates of key project documents? Your search is over!

Just pick this book up, and within minutes, you will not only know which meeting to set up to move your project forward, you will have easy-to-use templates of project documents that help you organize and execute your project. Here's what this book will do for you the moment you open it:

- Provide you with simple language to demystify the components of a project.
- Provide you with candid advice on the key meetings you need to set up to help a project succeed.
- Provide you with a basic refresher on how to set up and conduct an effective meeting.
- Provide you with easy-to-read examples in a business context, so you know how to relate it to your project.
- Provide you with templates so you can quickly create documents for your project.

From novice first-time project planners to the most seasoned project managers and other leaders, "*A Week in the Life*" will save you time as you plan and execute your projects. Remember, you don't have to have Project Management in your title to be responsible for project delivery in your organization. If you plan and implement activities at all levels, this book will help you. For more information, logon to www.yourpmassistant.com or email Janice and/or Brenda at info@yourpmassistant.com.

About the Authors

Janice Y. Rodgers, PMP

A California native, Janice Rodgers began her project management career as a software engineering officer in the US Air Force. She led many teams in the Air Force and used the PMI project management practices throughout her career. After she left the military,

Janice went on to begin her consulting career, which focused on managing software development projects and executing program management principles and practices. More details can be found online at:

http://www.linkedin.com/pub/janice-rodgers-pmp/0/796/692.

After using PMI practices for over ten years in her professional career, Janice decided to get her PMP® certification to further enhance her expertise and job performance. Recently, Janice finished an SAP business-transformation project, where she led a sales and marketing team to implement SAP using PMI® practices with the Advanced SAP methodology. Her expertise and practical applications of the PMI methodology is proven and extensive over her 20-year career.

Brenda K. Williams, PMP

An Ohio native, Brenda K. Williams began her project management career working for Fortune 500 companies and consulting firms in the field of project management. She received her PMP® certification from PMI® in 2005.

Brenda managed software development projects and executed program management initiatives at major corporations throughout the United States throughout her extensive career. Recently, Brenda finished an SAP business-transformation project, where she led a finance team to implement SAP using PMI practices with the Advanced SAP methodology. More details can be found online at: www.linkedin.com/in/brendakwilliams.

Active in the community, Brenda is a past president and current member of AWC (Association for Women in Computing), and member of both MPA (Microsoft Project Association) and PMI (Project Management Institute, Inc.).

Brenda received the 2007 Woman of Excellence Award from the Federation of Houston Professional Women.

Thank you for supporting Your PM Assistant!

Visit us for FREE project templates:

www.yourPMassistant.com

~~~

Need a meeting speaker?

Contact us:

info@yourPMassistant.com